27.07

What's Going On in the COMPOST PILE?

A Book About Systems

Rachel Chappell

Rourke
Publishing LLC

Vero Beach, Florida 32964

www.rourkepublishing.com

PHOTO CREDITS: Title Page: © Pattie Calfy; Page 5: © Norman Chan, Prism68, Vadim Kozlovsky, Alexander Remy Levine; Page 6: © Jenny Horne; Page 7: © Pilar Echevarria; Page 8: © Sebastion Kaulitzki, Florin Tirlen; Page 10: © Phil Morley; Page 11: © Donald Barger; Page 13: © Armentrout; Page 14: © Morgan Lane Photography; Page 15: © Jeff Gynane; Page 17: © Armentrout; Page 18: © Armentrout; Page 19: © Dennis Oblander; Page 21: © Eugene Bochkarev; Page 22: © Alison Cornford-Matheson

Editor: Robert Stengard-Olliges

Cover design by Michelle Moore.

Library of Congress Cataloging-in-Publication Data

Chappell, Rachel M. 1978-
  What's going on in the compost pile? : a book about systems / Rachel Chappell.
     p. cm. -- (Big ideas for young scientists)
  ISBN 978-1-60044-541-5 (Hardcover)
  ISBN 978-1-60044-702-0 (Softcover)
  1. Compost--Juvenile literature. I. Title.
  S661.C43 2008
  631.8'75--dc22
                                        2007018239

Printed in the USA

CG/CG

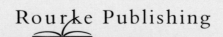

Rourke Publishing

www.rourkepublishing.com – rourke@rourkepublishing.com
Post Office Box 3328, Vero Beach, FL 32964

Table of Contents

Why Should You Compost?   4
Why Is a Compost Pile a System?   8
How Do You Create a Compost Pile?   12
Glossary   23
Index   24

Why Should You Compost?

The world needs all of us to compost! Everyday we throw away lots of stuff that really isn't trash. Things such as newspapers, cans, milk jugs, banana peels, and dried leaves should be **recycled** instead of thrown out.

When we recycle paper

it can be used to make paper or cardboard.

When we recycle plastic

it can be used to make park benches, fences, and furniture.

When we recycle tires

it can be used to make playground mats, chips and door mats.

When we recycle yard trash

it can be used to make fertilizer for soil.

    A **compost pile** is a heap of **decaying organic** matter. Organic matter is anything that comes from plants such as grass clippings, wood chips, watermelon rinds, or apple cores.

When we make a compost pile, we are recycling organic stuff. Adding recycled organic matter to soil makes it better for plants.

 Another name for composted stuff is "black gold" because this earthy smelling mixture is a treasure to soil and plants.

Why Is a Compost Pile a System?

A **system** is a group of parts that work together to perform a function. Each part in a system affects the other parts.

Other Systems in Nature

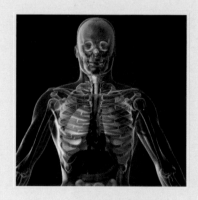

Human Body

Solar System

Beehive

A compost pile is a system with many parts and has the **function** of breaking down organic stuff. Bugs, slugs, worms, bacteria, dried leaves, kitchen scraps, air, and moisture all work together in a compost pile.

   You might be wondering how a compost pile works as a system. Bugs, slugs, and worms eat some of the organic matter. **Microorganisms** grow in the compost pile and eat matter too. Their wastes also add to the compost.

When worms, slugs, and insects move around inside the compost pile their tunnels help get air into the pile. All the organisms that are breaking down the plant material need air to do their jobs. Over time all the organic matter decays and becomes compost.

How Do You Create a Compost Pile?

It's easy to make a compost pile. Follow these simple steps to create a compost pile and help the environment. The first thing you do to build your compost pile is to collect the tools you will need.

Tools for composting

shovel

garden hose

gloves

compost bin

Then, you should decide where to put your compost pile. Place the compost bin somewhere outside, away from your house. But where your garden hose will reach it.

Now it's time to start filling your compost bin.

So what should you put in the compost bin? Brown stuff and green stuff are the two main ingredients you need for your compost pile.

Brown stuff	Green stuff
dead leaves, pine needles, small amounts of newspaper, and twigs	plants or grass clippings, weeds, fruit and vegetable scraps, coffee grounds, and eggshells

Lots of the green stuff comes from your kitchen scraps. But be careful, not all kitchen scraps are good for composting. Leave out meat scraps, milk, cheese, bones, and oils. They'll make your compost pile smell and attract animals and bugs.

Layering the ingredients in the compost pile is important.

Building a compost pile from the ground up.

Layer four - more brown stuff

Layer three - soil

Layer two - green stuff

Layer one - brown stuff

Wet ground under pile

Every few days you should stir, or turn over, your pile. This will spread out the microorganisms and worms. You can also keep adding brown and green stuff to your pile.

Turn over the compost to get more air in.

Over the next few months as the organisms in your compost system are at work, your pile will probably shrink in size.

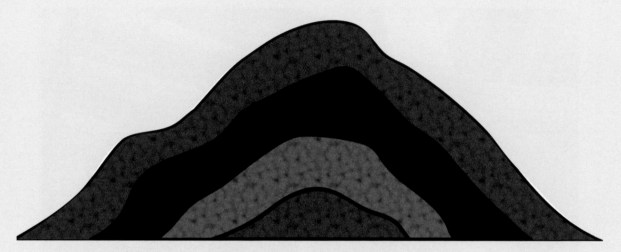

One month old.

Six months old.

The green and brown stuff decay and become dark, crumbly compost. Now this rich compost is ready to fertilize the plants in your yard and garden.

The environment needs you—let's compost!

Glossary

compost pile (KOM pohst pahyl) — a heap of organic material from yard and kitchen waste that is decayed and used for fertilizing soil

decay (di KAY) — to rot or break down

function (FUHNGK shuhn) — a purpose, role or job

microorganism (mye kroh OR guh niz uhm) — a living thing too small to be seen without a microscope

organic (or GAN ik) — material from living organisms like plants and animals

recycle (re SYE kuhl) — to treat or process waste materials so they are used again

system (SIS tuhm) — a whole unit made up of smaller parts

Index

decays   6, 11, 21
fertilize   5, 21
ingredients   16, 18
organic   6, 7, 9, 10, 11
soil   5, 7, 18
systems   8, 9, 10, 20
worms   9, 10, 11, 19

Further Reading

Koontz, Robin. *Composting: Nature's Recyclers*. Picture Window Books, 2007.

Scott, Nicky. *Little Green Guide to Composting*. Chelsea Green Publishing, 2007.

Websites to Visit

www.camrose.com/kids_camrose/composting
www.civicgardencenter.org/HTML/compkids.html

About the Author

Rachel M. Chappell graduated from the University of South Florida. She enjoys teaching boys and girls as well as their teachers. She lives in Sarasota, Florida and gets excited about reading and writing in her spare time. Her family consists of a husband, one son, and a dog named Sadie.